Introduction

FOR ANYONE JUST STARTING OUT, THESE RECIPES ARE THE EVERYDAY DISHES THAT FILL MY KITCHEN. AFTER TEN YEARS OF COOKING, I'VE LEARNED THAT ANYONE CAN FEEL AT HOME IN THE KITCHEN. THESE AREN'T FANCY MEALS OR CHEF-LEVEL TRICKS—JUST SIMPLE DISHES THAT TEACH YOU THE BASICS AND HELP YOU GROW. WISHING YOU THE BEST AS YOU BEGIN YOUR COOKING JOURNEY.

-DOM

Table of CONTENTS

Appetizers

TWENTY-FOUR RECIPES FROM BREAKFAST TO DINNER

Bruschetta

 4 servings   30 minutes

INGREDIENTS

- A roll of french bread
- handful of basil
- 5 cherry tomatoes
- 1 hot house tomato
- 2 tbsp olive oil
- a half piece of garlic
- Balsamic vinegar glaze

DIRECTIONS

1. Cut the bread into even slices.
2. Drizzle each side with olive oil and broil until lightly crisp.
3. Dice tomatoes and remove the watery center.
4. Slice basil and mix with tomatoes in olive oil. Let sit for 30 minutes in a small bowl.
5. Rub garlic on warm bread.
6. Add the tomato mix and top with a little balsamic glaze.
7. Enjoy.

Garlic bread

---

 4 servings   15 minutes

INGREDIENTS

- 1 loaf of french bread
- 1 roll of garlic butter
- a hand full of Pecorino Romano Cheese

DIRECTIONS

1. Prepare slices for everyone.
2. Toast each side until pale gold.
3. Brush with melted butter and top with cheese.
4. Toast again until the top is golden.
5. Serve and enjoy.

INGREDIENTS

- 1 package of hot dogs
- 2 packages of Pillsbury pizza dough

Pigs in a blanket

 4 servings   15-20 minutes

DIRECTIONS

1. Slice the hot dogs into small bites.
2. Break the dough into strips for wrapping.
3. Wrap each bite and set them on a baking tray.
4. Bake until lightly golden.
5. Enjoy fresh from the oven.

Buttery Garlic Dinner rolls

 4 servings   15 minutes

INGREDIENTS

- 2 tbsp of butter(melted)
- 24 pack of a Kings Hawaiian Rolls
- Handful of Pecorino Romano Cheese
- 1 tbsp parsley

DIRECTIONS

1. Melt butter using the microwave or a small pot on the stove.
2. Set the rolls on a non-stick pan and coat the tops with butter.
3. Top with grated cheese and a light shake of parsley.
4. Broil briefly until golden, watching carefully.
5. Remove, cool, then enjoy.

Breakfast

TWENTY-FOUR RECIPES FROM BREAKFAST TO DINNER

Bacon Egg and Cheese bagel

 1 servings 15 minutes

INGREDIENTS

- 2 eggs
- 1 everything bagel
- 2 slices of cheese
- 2 pieces of bacon

DIRECTIONS

1. Prepare the eggs and crisp the bacon.
2. Toast the bagel and add butter.
3. Warm the bacon, cover with cheese, and melt.
4. Add the cheesy bacon to the toasted bagel.
5. Serve and enjoy.

Breakfast Bowl

 4 servings   15 minutes

INGREDIENTS

- 2 cup of white potatoes
- 2 cups of frozen sausage
- 4 eggs
- 1.5 cups of cheese

DIRECTIONS

1. Cut the potatoes into cubes and place them in a pan with oil.
2. Add seasoning and cook the potatoes until they turn golden.
3. Scramble the eggs and blend in the sausage crumbles.
4. Sprinkle cheese over the warm egg and sausage mix.
5. Mix everything until it becomes creamy and fluffy.
6. Fill a bowl with the potatoes and add the egg mix on top.
7. Enjoy your meal!

Main Dishes

TWENTY-FOUR RECIPES FROM BREAKFAST TO DINNER

Sticky Wings

 2 servings   1.25 Hours

INGREDIENTS

- 20 wings
- a quarter cup of red vinegar
- a quarter cup of olive oil
- 2 pinches of onion powder
- 2 pinches of garlic powder
- ¾ cups of parsley

DIRECTIONS

1.Clean the wings and place them in a large bowl.

2.Add all the ingredients and chill for one hour to let the flavors soak in.

3. Set the oven to 375 and bake the wings in a metal tray, uncovered, for about an hour and 15 minutes until golden and ready to enjoy.

Chicken Parmesan

 6 servings   30 minutes

INGREDIENTS

- 8 thin boneless chicken cutlets
- 1 handful of Pecorino Romano Cheese
- 4 eggs
- A jar of pasta sauce
- seasoned italian bread crumbs
- 1 tbsp Parsley
- A pinch of pepper
- A pinch of salt
- 2 cups of mozzarella cheese shredded

DIRECTIONS

1. Beat the eggs in one bowl and mix the cheese and bread crumbs in another.
2. Warm your skillet and add enough corn oil to shallow fry.
3. Set the heat to medium-high and wait for the oil to shimmer.
4. Dip each chicken piece in the egg, then coat in the crumb mix.
5. Fry for about three minutes on each side until golden.
6. Move the chicken to the oven, add sauce and cheese, and broil until the cheese melts.
7. Serve and enjoy.

Chicken Francese

 4 servings   30 minutes

INGREDIENTS

- 8 palm sized chicken cutlets
- 1/4 cup all purpose flour
- 3 eggs
- 3 tbsp of whole milk
- 1/4 inch of olive oil in pan
- 1 lemon cut in slices
- 3 tbsp of unsalted butter
- 2 tbsp of all purpose flour
- 2 cups of beef broth
- 1/3 cup of Chardonnay or dry white wine
- pinch of pepper
- parsley flakes
- pinch of salt

DIRECTIONS

1. Prepare the chicken by cutting and pounding it.
2. Combine milk and eggs in one bowl and set the dry mix in separate bowls.
3. Dip the chicken into egg, then flour, then egg again for a crisp texture.
4. Cook the chicken on medium heat until golden on both sides.
5. Toast lemon slices in the same skillet and remove when browned.
6. Wipe out the skillet, melt butter, and blend in the flour.
7. Add wine and slowly add broth, letting the sauce simmer until slightly thick.
8. Add lemon slices and return the chicken to coat it fully.
9. Serve with potato chips and yellow rice for a bright, tasty finish.

pan seared steak

 2 servings   15 minutes

INGREDIENTS

- 1 boneless ribeye
- A sprig of thyme
- A sprig of rosemary
- 2 crush garlic cloves
- 4 tbsp of unsalted butter

DIRECTIONS

1. Heat the pan on medium and melt the butter with the oil.
2. Season the steak with salt and pepper.
3. Add the steak to the pan and keep spooning the hot butter over the top every few minutes.
4. Add the crushed garlic, herbs, and more butter as the steak finishes.
5. Let the steak soak up the flavor briefly, then set it aside to rest.
6. Slice, serve, and enjoy.

Porkchops

 4 servings   20 minutes

INGREDIENTS

- 4 boneless center cut pork chops
- 2 tbsp ground sage
- 2 tbsp dry rosemary
- 2 tbsp dry thyme leaves
- 2 tbsp olive oil
- 3 tbsp of unsalted butter

DIRECTIONS

1. Heat a pan on medium and drop in the butter.
2. Lay the pork chops on a plate and coat them with the dry spices.
3. Fry the pork chops and spoon the pan liquid over them now and then.
4. Cook until the pork turns a warm golden color.
5. Serve with any veggie you like and enjoy.

Philly Cheesesteak

 3 servings 20 minutes

INGREDIENTS

- 1.5 pounds of shaved fresh ribeye
- ¾ pounds of provolone cheese
- 3 mini hero rolls
- 1 whole sweet onion
- 3 tbsp of corn oil

DIRECTIONS

1. Take the meat out of the package and place it in a hot pan on medium-high heat.
2. In a second pan, brown the onion until soft and golden.
3. Mix the onion into the meat once it's cooked and no longer greasy.
4. When the meat is halfway done, stir in half of the cheese.
5. Add the meat and onions to the sandwich.
6. Serve right away so it stays warm.

Smash Burgers

 4 servings   15 minutes

INGREDIENTS

- 1.25 lbs ground beef
- salt & pepper
- 2 pinches garlic powder
- 2 pinches onion powder
- 4 burger buns
- 4 slices cheese (any kind you like)
- lettuce
- tomato (sliced)
- 4 Tbsp mayonnaise (or any favorite sauce)
- 3 Tbsp mayonnaise
- 1 Tbsp ketchup
- 8 pickles

DIRECTIONS

1. Make the sauce: Mix together mayo, ketchup, Stir well and chill in the fridge until ready to serve.
2. Form the patties: In a bowl, combine ground beef, salt, garlic powder, onion powder, paprika, salt, and pepper. Mix gently (don't overwork it). Divide into 4 equal portions and shape into patties slightly larger than your buns (they shrink when cooked!).
3. Cook the burgers: Heat a grill pan or skillet over medium-high heat. Ball up and press the patties down for 3–4 minutes per side. In the last minute of cooking, place a slice of cheese on each patty and cover with a lid to melt.
4. Toast the buns: Slice the buns and toast them cut-side-down in a dry pan or on the grill until golden brown.
5. Assemble your burger: Spread special sauce on both sides of the bun. Stack with lettuce, the cheesy patty, tomato, onion, pickles, and top bun. Press gently and serve hot.

Sunday Sauce

 12 servings   1.5 hours

INGREDIENTS

- 2 tbsp of tomato paste
- ¼ cup of italian seasoning
- 1 package of sweet sausage links
- 1 pound of chop meat
- 1 cup of onion
- fresh basil
- 3 bay leaves
- 1 tbsps oregano
- 2 tbsp of butter
- corn starch(if watery)
- 1 can of 28oz of plum tomatoes
- 1 can of 28oz of sauce
- 1 can of 28oz of crushed tomatoes

Meatballs

- 1 egg
- .5 cup of onion
- ½ cup of breadcrumbs
- 2 pounds of chop meat

DIRECTIONS

1. Set a large pot over medium heat. Add olive oil, onion, and ground meat, cooking until the onion softens and the meat browns.
2. Prepare the meatball mixture and roll into balls.
3. Bake the sausage and meatballs at 375 for roughly half an hour.
4. Pour in all sauces and seasoning and simmer for about an hour and fifteen minutes.
5. Brown the sausage and meatballs and add them to the pot.
6. Allow the sauce to cook until everything blends well.
7. Serve and enjoy with pasta or rice.

Pasta With Sage Butter

 2 servings   30 minutes

INGREDIENTS

- 4 fresh sage
- 2 tbsp of pasta water (use discretion)
- ¾ pounds bowtie pasta
- 4 tbsp unsalted butter
- a handful of graded, freshly Pecorino Romano Cheese.

DIRECTIONS

1. Cook the pasta in a pot of boiling water.
2. Gently melt the butter and let it brown while stirring.
3. Add the sage and warm it just until fragrant.
4. Mix in some cheese, then add the pasta.
5. Toss until everything comes together.
6. Serve warm and enjoy.

3 cheese mac and cheese

 6 servings   30 minutes

INGREDIENTS

- 1 cup of Gouda
- 1 cup of Fontina
- 1 cup of Cheddar
- 1 pound of elbow
- ¼ cup heavy cream
- 2 tbsp of unsalted butter
- ½ cup of Breadcrumbs

DIRECTIONS

1. Boil the pasta until Al Dente
2. Warm a pan and melt the butter.
3. Add the three cheeses one at a time, mixing slowly so they melt smoothly.
4. Pour in the heavy cream little by little once the cheese is fully melted.
5. Stir in the cooked pasta until everything is mixed.
6. Sprinkle breadcrumbs on top and broil until golden, keeping an eye so it doesn't dry out.
7. Serve right away.

INGREDIENTS

- 8 thin boneless chicken cutlets
- 4 eggs
- 2 cups Panko Crumbs
- 2 cups of all purpose flour
- 1 tbsp Parsley
- a pinch of pepper
- a pinch of salt
- Vegetable oil

Chicken Katsu

 6 servings   20 minutes

DIRECTIONS

1. Whisk the eggs in a bowl.
2. Fill one bowl with flour and another with bread crumbs.
3. Warm the oil in a skillet until it shimmers.
4. Dip the chicken in the egg, then coat it in the crumbs.
5. Fry for about three minutes on each side until crisp and golden.
6. Serve with kimchi.

Easy Stir Fry

 2 servings   20 minutes

DIRECTIONS

1. Place chopped chicken in a bowl with oil and Shaoxing wine. Chill for a few hours.
2. Soak rice in cold water, then rinse.
3. Cook veggies in a warm wok with a small amount of oil.
4. Simmer rice in water with a touch of butter and oil until tender.
5. Add chicken to the hot wok and stir while you add soy sauce.
6. Add veggies back in with a small splash of soy and cook quickly.
7. Serve and enjoy.

INGREDIENTS

- 1 pound of chicken breast
- ½ cup of Corn starch
- splash Soy sauce
- ½ cup of Vegetable oil
- 1 tbsp of butter
- 1 tbsp of olive oil
- 1 tbsp of Shaoxing wine
- Mixed vegetables of choice
- 1.5 cup of white rice

Corn Dogs

 6 servings   20 minutes

INGREDIENTS

- 12 hot dogs
- 6 mini hot dogs
- 1 tbsp of baking powder
- 1 egg
- A pinch of pepper
- A pinch of salt
- 1/4 cup of sugar
- 1 3/4 cups of buttermilk
- 1 tbsp of honey
- 1 1/2 cups of fine yellow corn meal
- 1 tbsp of vegetable oil
- 6 tooth picks
- 12 skewers
- 2-4 quarts of Corn oil

DIRECTIONS

1. Heat corn oil in a Dutch oven until it reaches 350 degrees.
2. Pat all hot dogs dry and add skewers.
3. Combine dry ingredients in one bowl and wet in another.
4. Stir everything together and pour into a tall glass.
5. Dip each hot dog into the batter until fully covered.
6. Fry in the hot oil, rotating as needed.
7. Remove when golden brown.
8. Cool and serve.

Tacos

 4 servings   20 minutes

INGREDIENTS

- 2 pounds of sirloin
- 2 tbsp of chili powder
- 1 1/2 tsp of cumin
- 1 tsp of dried oregano
- 1/2 tsp garlic powder
- 1/2 tsp onion powder
- 1 cup of tomato sauce
- 10 soft tortilla wraps
- Vegetable oil

DIRECTIONS

1. Cook the meat on high until fully browned.
2. Drain fat and return meat to the pan.
3. Stir in seasoning and tomato sauce.
4. Simmer for a short time.
5. Heat oil in a cast iron pan and warm a tortilla.
6. Add cheese, cook for a moment, and fold once golden.
7. Add the meat and any extras you like.
8. Serve hot and enjoy.

Side Dishes

TWENTY-FOUR RECIPES FROM BREAKFAST TO DINNER

Mexican Street Corn Slaw

 4 servings   15 minutes

INGREDIENTS

- 1 pack of sweet corn
- A hand full Cotija cheese
- splash of lime juice
- 1 tbsp chili powder
- vegetable oil

DIRECTIONS

1. Heat a pan on medium and cook the corn until tender.
2. Combine the chili powder while the corn steams.
3. Stir the cooked corn with mayo and a little lime.
4. Add Cotija cheese or use as a taco topping.
5. Enjoy.

potato and butternut squash bites

 4 servings   40 minutes

INGREDIENTS

- 1 package of boiler potatoes
- 1 package of cut up butternut squash
- splash olive oil
- 2 tbsp of unsalted butter
- generous amount of italian seasoning

DIRECTIONS

1. Cut the potatoes and squash into small pieces. Toss them in a pan with olive oil and your favorite seasonings.
2. Place the pan in the oven at a 425 and add a few small pieces of butter around the pan.
3. Give everything a gentle flip now and then. Remove when the edges look golden and slightly dark.
4. Serve warm and enjoy.

Cilantro Lime Rice

 2 servings   15 minutes

INGREDIENTS

- 1 lime
- 1 bushel of cilantro
- 1 cup of white rice
- 1 tbsp of salted butter
- 1 tbsp of olive oil

DIRECTIONS

1. Boil water, then add butter and a little oil.
2. Add the rice and let it simmer until fluffy.
3. Stir in the cilantro and lime.
4. Serve right away so it stays soft.

Sweet potato mash

 4 servings   15 minutes

INGREDIENTS

- 4 sweet potatoes
- 2 tbsps of unsalted butter

DIRECTIONS

1. Quarter the potatoes and place them in boiling water until soft.
2. Drain the water and return the potatoes to the pot.
3. Melt the butter into the potatoes and mash until smooth.
4. Serve and enjoy.

www.ingramcontent.com/pod-product-compliance
Lightning Source LLC
Chambersburg PA
CBHW041620120626
46551CB00003B/518